POETIC MOMENTS IN PSYCHOTHERAPY

POETIC MOMENTS IN PSYCHOTHERAPY

BRYAN C. HAZELTON, LCSW, CASAC, BCD

abbott press®

A DIVISION OF WRITER'S DIGEST

Abbott Press books may be ordered through booksellers or by contacting:

Abbott Press
1663 Liberty Drive
Bloomington, IN 47403
www.abbottpress.com
Phone: 1-866-697-5310

Because of the dynamic nature of the Internet, any web addresses or links contained in this book may have changed since publication and may no longer be valid. The views expressed in this work are solely those of the author and do not necessarily reflect the views of the publisher, and the publisher hereby disclaims any responsibility for them.

ISBN: 978-1-4582-1060-9 (sc)
ISBN: 978-1-4582-1059-3 (e)

Library of Congress Control Number: 2013912566

Printed in the United States of America.

Abbott Press rev. date: 7/26/2013

Dedication

I am dedicating this book to my 10th generation
Great-Grandparents,
Anthony Thacher and Elizabeth Jones Thacher.
They harrowingly survived the Great Storm of 1635.
A first hand report of their sad losses and most
unimaginable experience can be found online at

The Shipwreck of Anthony Thacher

Introduction

It is my pleasure to present to you,

"Poetic Moments in Psychotherapy."

Nearly all of these poems were directly inspired by my work as a psychotherapist. Although I had 25 years of practice with no thought to write poetry, the poems and this book naturally emerged over the last several years. Similar to the process of psychotherapy where a session naturally evolves through a sense of freedom and trust, this book came into being.

Building Empathy

I construct the patient's world within me,

beam by feel,

floor by thought.

Positioning of doors.

Thickness of walls.

Visibility through windows.

When erected,

I'll know what it's like to live there.

The Prime Directive

We connect,

while removing ourselves,

to clarify them.

Crisscrossing

My patient fashioned crisscrossing causeways

across a rising body of water.

Will that many roads be necessary?

Tick Tock

Patient talks.

I respond by facial cues.

I grasp the deeper meaning.

They both exist on either side of the instant.

United by intuition.

Transferential Lighting

Present ... future ... past ... present ...
time-shadows flicker upon the face of experience.
Visible and then not, they tumble and shift,
while fluttering in and out of the container
known as
now.

Timeless

Vast wastelands of silent space
spinning in their emptiness,
as the mind-numbing nothingness
rings in the sickening void.
A tumbleweed rolls by as my patient crosses his leg.

Receiving

Paths to the heart, roads of the mind.

Appear in front of me all the time.

I hold to myself within their light,

to see the darkness that burdens their night.

Hearts and minds follow their course.

I match the mix,

while seeking the source.

Red lights, green lights, coming at me,

I choose what they choose, in order to see.

Fasten

I shook him up.

Now let him be.

Let it settle.

Then look and see.

Did he keep it?

Or did it go?

Build upon it?

I don't quite know.

I'll be looking,

for signs ahead.

That he took it.

But it went unsaid.

I can visit

and try again.

If not today,

maybe when . . .

Numbers

27 minutes down,

18 to go.

6th of the day,

5 more after.

23rd of the week,

41 scheduled.

Most recent of 44,750+

Limit the numb.

Artless

The patient talks on, suddenly a few select words
capture my attention. They echo within me.
As each is spun, it is reviewed internally. If the
volume and speed of the echoing words increases,
I stop and explore.

If not,

the echo will fade

and my interests will shift back to

the whole.

Etching The Possibilities

As my Patient talked on, the constructed shell of
what he might be experiencing expanded in size.
I envisioned blueprint-like sketches on a black
sky. Increasing, without clarification, the range
of possibilities grew significantly. I found myself
hoping for clarity to arrive, as holding all the
various ideas with their attached emotion, began
to be too weighty. The stress of the structure had
nearly reached full capacity. I then recalled that
the building of New York City was possible due to
the underpinning of bedrock as its foundation.

A timely and fortifying association.

The Aesthetic Movements of Avoid

By the middle of the session it had been established.

A space place had taken a square shape.

Four flowers turned and twirled within, brushing upon the center

Planted there, was a palette where

words and meaning briefly fared.

Then peeling and fading,

with a fleetness, not saying.

Showing,

without revealing.

Compulsive Liar

How sad.

I sense a thin layer of absorbent gauze.

It braces me for the wound of the next emerging breach.

I strive for empathy,

he strives to not be known.

Direction

Square platform, close walls, surrounded by four doors.

A fast paced floor flashing of light,

then dark and then

light again.

The doors: truth or lies, substance abuse or recovery.

How do I get through?

Not through the doors, through to him about the doors.

My choice affects his.

They both define all moments going forward.

His Narrative

A series of pieces, united they're not.

Erecting the sides, but minus a top.

Leaning with meaning, then shifting the shape.

Arranging then changing, patterns quite late.

Black and white views, that colorfully clash.

As hope for emotion is held hostage and dashed.

Is this his world or is it a disguise?

I'll seek out the truth, by earth and by skies.

I'll strive for the heart, questing his view.

To know what is right, what's true and what's *new.*

That it's his, I must, respect all the way,

only then might he be open, choosing to say . . . .

Building His Structure of "I Am."

There is no roof and he has no hat.

Open space moves beneath his feet.

Confusing walkways that precipitously drop.

Rain and wind coldly buffet his balance.

No handholds to steady.

waiting

To pour a foundation,

while patching walls.

Painting will come later,

platforms are pre-floors.

A staircase imagined . . .

Suddenly, it becomes all about a door,

and which side he's on.

Omitted

I am sitting and listening

when suddenly sputtering holes of non-hear,

edit my receptivity.

Staccato-like, they leave the whole perforated with

cylinders of

Nothing

Patients issues aside, this is mine.

Psychotherapeutic Utensils

Sponge

Mirror

Sifter

Knife

Scale

Blender

Timer

Loco-motive?

As I am following my patient's train of thought,

he suddenly diverts the direction

and hops onto another track.

I quickly replay his words in my mind,

so as to identify his departure location,

along with a possible destination.

Is this a traveling towards or away from the

relevant station?

Fractured Infusion

Suddenly, in session, the visual of my patient

fractured into

jigsaw pieces, in tight.

One piece, part patient and part surroundings,

blew like a manhole cover splitting into two at eye level,

framing my face and eyes.

A gaseous blast of angst escaped from both sides.

In an instant, balance was lost and then regained.

Next moment.

I Hear Voices

My internal voice, his external words.

Listening to the two.

Seeking the difference,

to clarify the who.

Hearing intently,

to know it so deep.

Knowledge to hold on to,

understandings to keep.

Plumbing the layers,

of him and of me.

Outside and inside,

in an effort to see.

It's not as easy,

as we think it to be.

Blurring can happen,

from that we're not free.

What Triggered This?

As we sat down, he spoke at rapid fire pace.

Words, rat-a-tat-tat, shot out from a revolving circle of supply.

Most of which went over my head, leaving me stunned and wounded.

The barrage continued as rounds of multiple meanings knocked me to the floor,

bleeding.

Slowly, I established a foothold by culling key words from his volley.

I mirrored them, giving me time to regain my seat,

as my wounds faded from

feel.

Am I Missing The Sky?

It was 2:25 and I was picking up my 1st grader at his school. Although the schoolyard was soon to be awash with young children's gleeful voices, I was bored. I happened to glance up and see a uniquely expressive

sky

A blessed blend of billowing white clouds, was patched onto a rich blue sky. Suddenly, I felt the shining sun burn through my being, filling me with brightness. Jolted back to reality, I realized I had overlooked the world around me. When the bell rang, my son bounded out the school door and I made it my business to not miss his sparkling eyes and the open sky in his smile.

Curiosity

As my patient is talking,

a stated phrase suddenly sails out to me.

I repeat it internally, not quite knowing why.

I turn it over in my mind,

like a child looks at a pretty stone.

It stays with me as I look at the contours

seeking the sparkle.

Like a flight at night, I search for the light

to land the reason this phrase became

airborne.

Mend a Leg

The stage is bare.

Then she appears.

Scenery unfolds, born a mere tear.

Others join her, but just where she puts them.

Words wrap around them, as color emerges.

The seats are empty, as I sit here alone.

She sees me as plenty, a thousand more told.

I miss her move and the stage becomes bare.

Intermission comes early, when I lose her share.

I look back again and her play springs alive,

joined with actions and meanings to derive.

Then, two tall folks with Hats, block my view.

Perhaps it's her script that induces me to

lose my touch, my connection with you.

I dream up the look and apply the spot,

Focusing it bright, to shed some new light.

Careful I am, to not be too near.

No reason to bring fright, it has its own fear.

It is hard Being,

on stage.

In The Quiet Shade

Sentences said, are like droplets of rain,

dripping from the leaves of her life.

They fall into the still pond of my being.

Each has its own impact,

as the ripples gently become part

of me.

Lucy

March 20, 2011

Brown leaves. Early spring.

Voluminous plumes of olfactory delights.

My dog feels understood,

when I speak her language.

On

Round and round on the surface it goes.

No one stops and no one knows.

Slipping on ice, shallow it be,

the heart is closed,

there's nothing to see.

From A to Z,

no emotion expressed.

No hope for meaning,

it's all repressed.

Imagine it though,

with the feelings so felt,

that the words melt away

and

I open my self.

I see what she says and now know how to be,

I free her from hurting,

and be there for me.

I Work in Sales

We are saleswomen and salesmen.

We sell Hope.

Hope that situations will improve.

Hope that certain feelings will change.

Hope that certain behaviors will cease.

Hope that the past can be left behind.

Hope that we'll have courage going forward.

Hope that the future will be better.

This has got to be a dream

I am in a big ballroom with hundreds and hundreds of people.
It is as if we are all guests at a wedding. Why do I feel I know
these people? Some I recognize, but cannot recall their names.
Others are hauntingly familiar. Suddenly in a flash, I realize
fully that I am with every Patient that I have ever worked with!
Remarkably, there's a feeling of absolute certainty that every
each of them is being their exact self at this moment. The
drinkers are drinking, the unstable are getting worked up,
the sad are sad, and the distant are withdrawing.
Perfection extends,
as I profoundly breathe their fullness, their humanity.
What is this?!

This has got to be a dream.

A-maze-d

A swarm of words surround and crowd.

They leave me jammed inside

a

thick, block-like maze

of no direction.

I search for surface as the hum and buzz engulfs.

Time lifts the haze,

as patience breeds the pattern,

unveiling

the

form.

Anxiety Attacks

Holes in the fabric.

Cross tying

the

past and present,

feelings and thoughts,

fears and wishes,

thickets a net.

Adaptation by holding.

Fred Astaire

How you glide and slide,

so smooth, so effortlessly.

You float like a feather on the edge of the wind.

Your Charm arrives on time, so naturally.

Your sublime footwork is only surpassed by your deft sidestep.

Your dance across the room ends with you further away.

Your beauty stands so tall that it conceals that which needs

attention.

You may not stumble, but I do, as I fall prey to your

gracefulness.

Now I admire, then look past the thin celluloid of your life.

I now understand that what pains you is hidden between takes.

Sit down. Let's talk.

8 Weeks Clean

Clearly triggered by something that happened,

(or didn't).

The magnetic pull intensified in tug, as the urge dug

deep.

Wafting through the barrier of his own solid sense

and respected reason,

the substance called to him.

His now-time need for soothing

swiftly moved along the rails of a resentment.

Action emerged.

By the third cigarette a short while later, he exclaimed:

"Hell, I'm smoking again . . ."

Balloon

As my patient is talking about his impending vacation,

I think of my own approaching.

I suddenly envision the painting on the wall grow a

tail and rise up towards the ceiling.

For Whom does the Balloon Rise?

Receptivity

I'm immersed in a tub of vicarious experience.

Bathed in emotion.

Conditions provided.

Floating optional, but preferred.

The Axis is Tilted

Imagine 9 chairs sitting outside the office door.
They're lined up next to each other in a row.
Resting on each seat is the earth, as it appears from the moon.
Although they are the same, what is visible differs from one to
another
Some are in daylight, others in the dark of night. Viewing each
reveals a diversity of features: unyielding masses of land,
jagged mountainous peaks forged by collision, and a multitude
of white swirling storms moving across deeply consuming
seas. A closer look discloses bridges linking islands and sound
ground with plowed furrows of promise. But sadly, one world
solely reveals a desolate and frozen polar cap.

A guide is evident on the front of each chair:

9:15, 10:15, 11:30, 1:15 . . .

Ah, I recognize this,

it's Tuesday.

Out, To Be In

As my patient spoke one sunny Friday in June,

I had a Mad powerful urge to jump up

and dial the clock forward!

I just had to act!!

My arms ached with restraint,

as I maintained being contained.

My time will soon be here, up around the bend, just

ahead . . .

Issac

His orbit brings him, swooping by,

looping from close, to very far.

Like a moon swinging on in,

only to swoop away, again.

Time to think and a moment to feel,

is left behind as the route is revealed.

Ovalling in its repetition,

I contrast his positions,

to

decipher his

Laws Of Motion.

Sew What?

Seeking the thread,

to find the line,

of what goes on,

inside his mind.

Words go on,

many they be.

But there's a theme,

I'm seeking to see.

Ideas of real,

are split in two.

As I assign with care,

the who is who.

Me or him,

it has to be.

One of us is you,

the other me.

I then act forward, as the view is shown,

Stitching the fabric, by the moment honed.

Augenblich

Envisioned and gone in an instant,

up popped like the weasel

a slightly smaller copy of my patient's head within his

own.

At that moment he had started to talk of his immediate

experience in session.

Imagine an Open Field

Acres and acres of flat prairie land.

Smack in the middle, a man faced toward the viewer,

stands behind a closed gate.

Peering through the posts he longs to get through, but

cannot.

The man stands transfixed.

He can't see the open horizon on both sides.

Joe 5:30 pm

White Horses Stride Into
The Black Night.

Intuition

Seeking a broad application.

Apply within.

Black Meets White

At the end of a long trying day,

I turn to complete my patient's notes.

There's so much to write and I'm worn from the jolting

day.

I imagine just tilting my head down,

and having words and sentences pour from my

forehead.

Black letters fluttering onto white paper.

Purpose and meaning, married by wish.

But no, I must administer my own ink.

I must remain available again, today, to each patient,

one by one, from last to first.

Feelings and thoughts, letters on a page.

And worlds to go, before I sleep.

Suddenly,

my

Patient,

had a burst of pride.

"I have so much to tell you!!"

I could feel the clusters of rich reddening affects

within his bosom.

They're Off

I am coming down the stretch,

racing to stay ahead of my tired and dissolving attention.

I have but minutes to go before the tape.

It is the last hour of my week's work

and I can't wait for the end to become.

Hold on! I tell the beast bucking within me.

But I am done.

My stride weakens with every word.

In the last few moments I lose control of my

tone

and

get

nosed out

at

the

wire.

Official results sadly show a second loss.

Cradling an Oval Plaque in Your Arms

On it are rows and columns of wall switches
in the standard on or off position.
We cradle with care the diverse assortment, as we assess
that some of the switches in
the on position would
best be off,
while others in the off position
should be on.

We are called upon to change select positions.

Turn off the on of drug abuse.
Turn on the light of self-awareness.
Darken the memory of traumatic events.
Turn on the capacity for hope.
Switch off self-defeating behaviors.

Yet, some fiercely stay stuck in place,
as the question constantly looms:
Am I addressing the right switch, at the right time?

Faux Session

A syrup-like, boundary-less,

soup of non-involvement.

A hazy hideout built for 1 and 1, by 2.

My patient and I joined

in an unexpected collusion to remain

separate.

Seenery

A swift shallow stream polishes giant oval boulders.

They lay scattered in a line to the horizon.

Silent in their stillness,

they rest beneath a white patched blue sky,

framed with bi-lateral greenery.

As time flows forward,

the session moves from rock to crevice,

from wet to deep.

I seek my path, but it prevents me from finding his.

I find my direction, but lose the way.

Looking in, I see that I haven't, and mend my sight.

Suddenly the water is still,

as the sky meets the stone,

and

colors, signal this seeker.

Weave 'em and Reap

Palettes of feeling. Palettes of thought.

Palettes of vision, that is what's sought.

Each has their own, varied they be,

culled from a theme and easy to see.

Put layer on layer, combine their being.

And shore up the spot,

Too painful to be in.

Penultimate few minutes

Suddenly, I imagine my patient as a black silhouette,

his double is opposite him,

and they're joined at the knee.

I untie the shoelace between one to the disparate other.

Its all I can do for now . . .

Poems are read slowly, read this Rap-it.

defences

the fences

are put up

to shut up

the voice of pain

when it rains

flooding the scene

when you can't believe

that the whole can be

you just can't see

what to do

to make it through

to find the prize

whatever size

to make the smile

and bake the file

that saws the bars

to free your soul

and make you whole

it's there

it's not rare

ya gotta see

you can surely be

You may feel a slight pinch

I'm snipping the edges.
Building the themes.
Absorbing the feelings.
Seeing what's to see.

I'm snipping the edges.
Not cutting too close.
Blotting the blood.
While measuring the dose.

I'm snipping the edges.
And hearing the here . . .
So stay with me,
trust me,
no reason for fear.
Just snipping the edges . . .

The Gallery

I walk, as the Patient talks.

I enter an Art Gallery

with numerous white bare adjoining rooms.

The patient paints a picture,

I construct the image.

They're seen, but only some are hung.

They fade and brighten, as their value shifts.

Some are chosen.

Some existed once.

Dark Corridor

A place for my Patient.
Unencumbered by the light of others or self.
Restricted by its limits,
broadened by rich individuality.

Out of the darkness and into my mind,
flies the meaning and name,
of each of his kind.

Friends, Family, Workmates, Villains.
Heroes, Victims, Lovers, and Mirrors.

The wealth of absence
grants finding, without seeking.
This bare cave of black
brings a richness of recall,
as I rest in their well of
wherever.

Prime Time

As the patient comes into the *living* room

of our office,

we open

the double doors of our engagement center.

They choose the channel,

as we allow their movie to play inside us.

Colors, shapes, interactions of every sort.

Life blazes on.

I can see and feel it on the screen within.

Adjust the dials by our involved distance, as we

seek

the

Clearest Picture.

Feel For The Day

This morning just before awakening,
I was blessed to feel the wonderful oneness of
Humanity
Expressions, smiles, the language of the body,
repeatedly voiced and felt, through the far, far ages,
of mankind past.
A clear feeling it was, yet the dream evaporated
like the dew on the May morning grass outside my
window.
My arm rises as I extend my hand to all those whose
cooperative connectedness kept the earth turning,
until this,
the turn of
You and I.